Maggots on the Menu

Contents

Written by Mike Gould

Collins

1 Insects on the menu

How did you feel when you read the title of this book? Did it make you feel queasy – or lick your lips? Perhaps that depends on whether you have ever knowingly eaten an insect.

Whatever your answer, the chances are that you – or someone you know – is *already* choosing insects as part of their diet.

If you already eat insects, you might know you can have them in burgers and cakes, in pasta and pancakes. Or as a special treat – just as they are, or dried and fried.

Love it or hate it, insect food is here to stay!

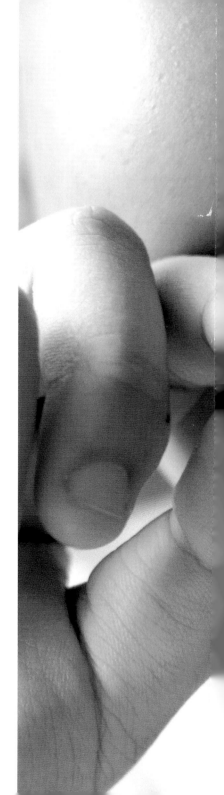

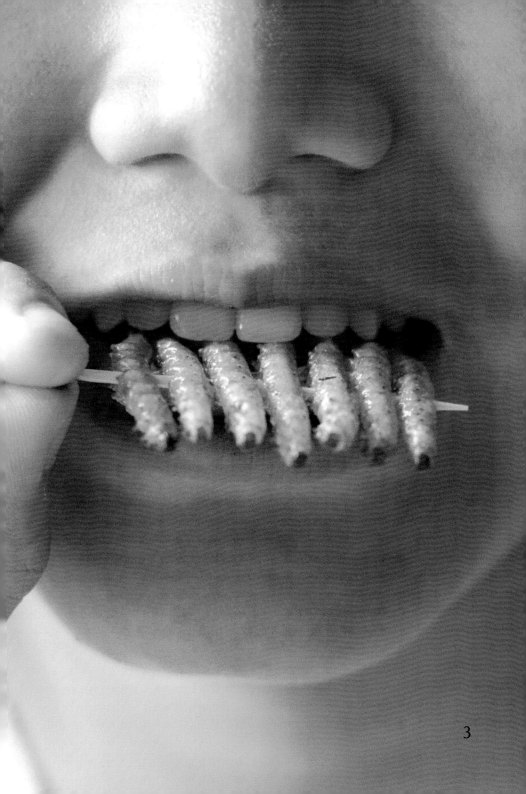

3

According to an organisation called the International Platform of Insects for Food and Feed (IPIFF), two billion people in over 80 per cent of countries in the world eat insects or insect products.

IPIFF also say that there are 2000 insect species around the world which they believe are edible.

These include mealworms, locusts, tarantulas and even scorpions!

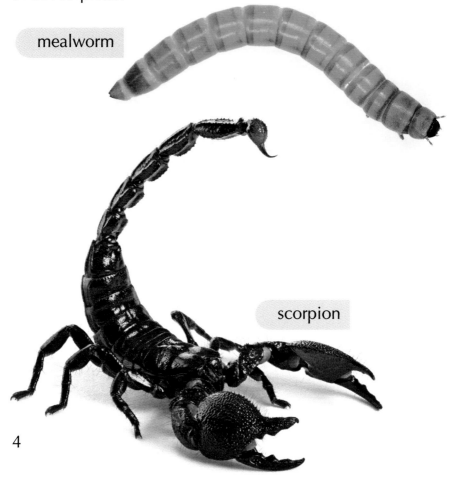

mealworm

scorpion

tarantula

edible locust

In fact, insects have been an important part of people's diets for thousands of years.

So, should we all be eating insects? Or are **maggots** on the menu a step too far for some people?

2 Entomophagy – what is it?

Eating insects is certainly not
unusual in the animal kingdom.
There, entomophagy is
a common practice.

The word "entomophagy" means
the practice of eating insects.
It comes from the Greek
"entomon" (insect) and
"phagein" (to eat) and applies
not just to humans who eat
insects but to any living
creatures that consume them.

You might already know the terms for meat-eaters (carnivores) and plant-eaters (herbivores). Those that eat both are omnivores.

Animals that eat insects are called insectivores.

Common examples of animals that eat insects include:

- reptiles, such as lizards and snakes
- many types of fish, such as carp and trout
- mammals, such as anteaters (the clue is in the name!), armadillos, sloth bears and marmosets
- birds, such as swallows and nightingales …

… and, not forgetting insects themselves! Insects, such as dragonflies, hornets and praying mantises all **devour** other insects.

For these creatures, insects are part of their primary diet. In other words, it is the main way they get the essential **nutrients** they need to survive.

For others, insects might not be their first choice of food, but eating insects provides them with **supplements** at important times, for example, during breeding.

3 Who eats insects?

If insects are good enough to eat for many animals, why not for us too?

Before humans had tools to hunt or farm, it is likely insects provided an important part of their diet. Cave paintings from Altamira in Spain, dating from 30,000 to 9000 BCE, show people collecting bee nests. It is thought that the humans of that time might have eaten the bee **larvae** as well as the honey.

There are many ancient Egyptian paintings which also show how important insects were.

For example, this picture shows honey being collected. Experts believe Egyptians probably ate insects too, although probably not live bees themselves!

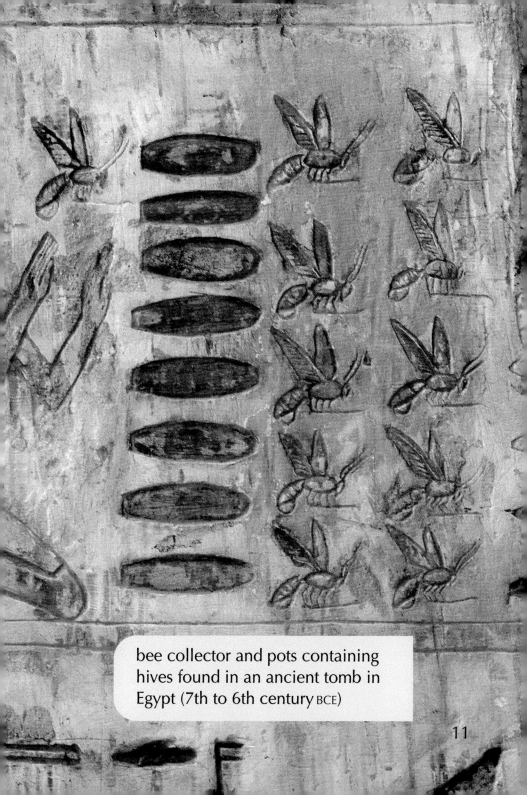

bee collector and pots containing hives found in an ancient tomb in Egypt (7th to 6th century BCE)

You might think that it was fine eating insects in the past, but what about today? Where do the estimated two billion people who eat insects come from?

Look at this map of the world. It shows some of the places where people eat insects.

Who eats bugs?

23 countries in
the Americas

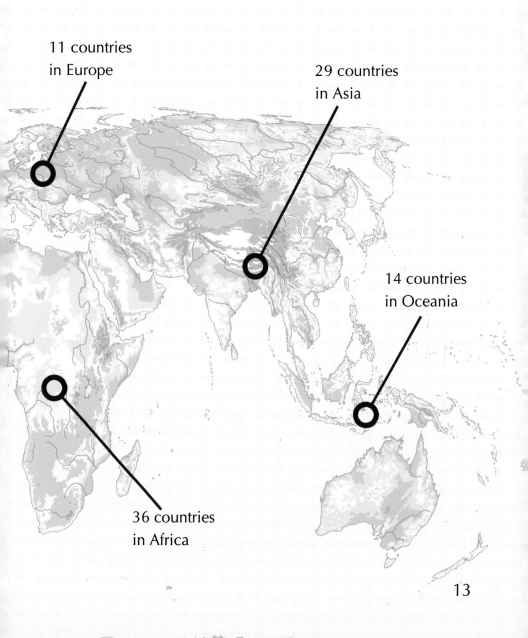

11 countries
in Europe

29 countries
in Asia

14 countries
in Oceania

36 countries
in Africa

4 So, what insects can you eat?

Check out this menu. Here are just a few of the ways that insects can be eaten.

Menu

Starters

Carrot buffalo worm soup

Boiled, dried caterpillar
– a fruity taster!

Roasted grasshopper
with chilli and lime
– crunchy, chicken taste

Mains

Fried tarantula in garlic
– a crunchy, slightly
nutty flavour

Scorpion skewers
– crispy, like French
fries, but healthier!

Gourmet bug burgers –
a mealworm, cricket and
grasshopper mix!

Health warning!

Do not try to eat or cook insects at home. Many insects contain harmful **toxins** that need to be removed, and even when cooked, you might be allergic to some of them.

Desserts

Wasp crackers – rather bitter, with the wasps giving a texture like raisins

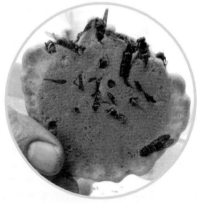

Chocolate ant cookies – dipped in chocolate, with a minty taste

Fried locusts – topped with meringue

5 Why are insects so tasty?

Like other foods, insects have a wide range of flavours.

For example, some ants have an acidic taste, rather like the sourness of lemon or lime.

Beetles, which have been used to create burgers in Denmark, have a strong umami flavour. This is savoury and salty, like a lot of meat.

Then, there is the texture. The crunch of many fried insects can be compared to popular snacks, such as peanuts, cheese crackers or sesame and prawn toasts. This is particularly true of insects with hard exoskeletons, like grasshoppers and crickets.

The exoskeleton is the hard covering which goes over the body of some insects.

In fact, there is probably an insect flavour or texture for everyone.

6 Is eating insects good for you?

Researchers think that some insect species provide as much, if not more, healthy nutrients than common animal food, such as chicken and beef.

For example, based on 100 grams:

A cricket	Minced beef
121 **calories**	200–300 calories (depending on how it is prepared)
12.9 grams of **protein**	23.5 grams of protein
5.5 grams of fat	21.2 grams of fat
5.1 grams of **carbohydrate**	0 grams of carbohydrate

Although beef has more protein, the fat and calorie content in the cricket is far lower.

Researchers also think insects may be very good at providing key vitamins. Crickets provide a good source of iron and vitamin B12. Iron can help build up resistance against infection, and vitamin B12 is helpful in maintaining healthy red blood cells. It can also prevent tiredness and lack of appetite.

7 Which insects are healthiest to eat?

There are many factors that explain which insects are healthiest to eat. However, if you look just at iron uptake (the amount of iron that you get from eating particular insects) then this chart gives you an idea.

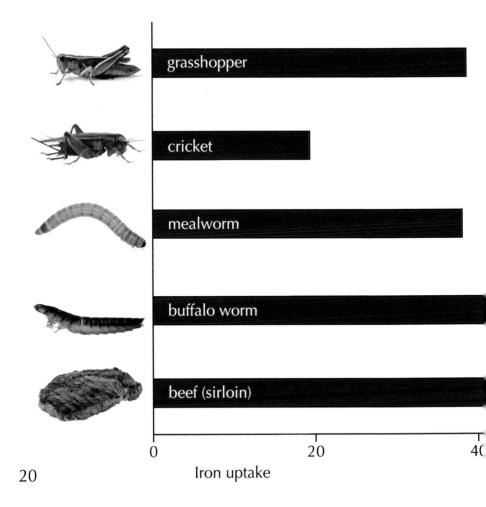

Iron uptake

So, according to this table, if you want
to keep up your energy levels
and perhaps reduce
the effects of coughs
and colds, then
a plate of (cooked)
buffalo worms
might be
the answer!

60   80   100

8 Solved! Insects to the rescue?

Organisations such as IPIFF (International Platform of Insects for Food and Feed) claim that insects can help solve many of the world's problems. They say that less land and water are needed to farm insects compared to cattle.

As the world's population grows, the demand for food grows. To meet this need, lots of forest and **scrub** has been cut down to create large farms for cattle or crops, such as wheat. This creates a number of problems. Firstly, it reduces biodiversity.

Biodiversity means having lots of different species of plants and animals in one area. If biodiversity is reduced, it means there are fewer species.

Secondly, forest and scrub is good for absorbing a harmful gas called carbon dioxide. If trees are destroyed, then such gases heat the atmosphere. These gases are often called "greenhouse gases" as they make Earth warmer. This in turn can lead to changes in the climate, such as increased flooding or drought.

Cattle feeding on farmland created by chopping down forest

9 How can insect farming help?

Cattle need a lot of feeding. As well as the shortage of land for farming cattle, there is also a shortage of animal feed. This feed is often made from large amounts of crops, such as soybeans and corn. So, could replacing some of these ingredients with insects help?

Experts argue that insects like maggots are already part of the natural diet of lots of animals. These include some fish and poultry – so it makes sense to use them to supplement animal feed.

But, it would need a big change in the way animal feed is produced – and a lot of insects would need to be harvested!

10 Cattle or crickets?

Many farmers are facing a problem: lack of land on which to grow crops or to graze cattle. So, why not create a different sort of farm?

Insect farming could produce a steady income for farmers. One type of insect which is well-suited to being farmed is the cricket.

Crickets are the insects which are farmed most around the world. This is because they have a high level of protein and are good for converting into foods like flour.

There are different ways of processing crickets, but one way involves baking and freezing them.

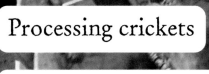

Processing crickets

1. First, the crickets are bred in a cricket farm like the one pictured below.

2. After seven weeks, they are slowly cooled down until they freeze. This is meant to be the most humane way of killing them.

3. Once they are frozen, they are then baked.

4. Finally, the crickets are ground into fine brown powder, like flour.

Crickets often live and breed in high-rise cartons in a hot and humid atmosphere. They are fed grains, fruit and vegetables.

11 Why *shouldn't* we eat insects?

Is insect farming as **sustainable** as it appears?

According to experts, some processes used in turning insects into food need a lot of energy, for example, for freezing or drying the insects.

They also say that if we start farming insects in huge numbers, we might affect other species. What happens to species that depend on insects for food if we take them all?

Then there is the question of whether it is right to eat insects.

Many people believe eating *any* living creature is wrong – eating insects is no better than eating chicken or beef.

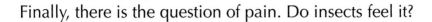

Finally, there is the question of pain. Do insects feel it?

In fact, an article in the *Smithsonian* magazine (a specialist science magazine) reported that after 15 years of research, some scientists found out that they do. When insects in their study suffered extreme heat or cold, they felt sudden pain (like when you cut your finger). Another experiment showed that if an insect had a damaged leg, for example, it also suffered chronic pain (pain that lasts a longer time, like if you tear a muscle).

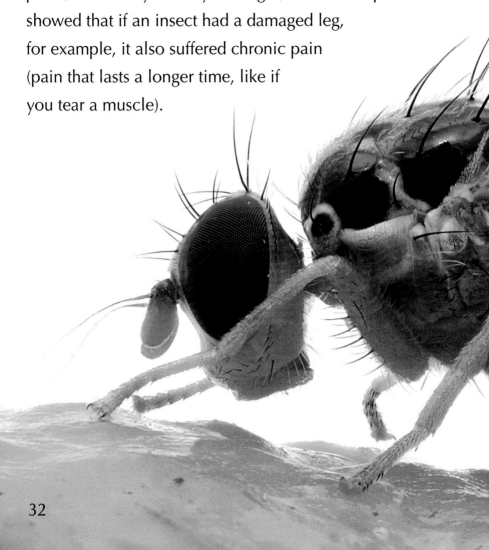

Just because insects are sometimes seen as creepy or ugly, is it right to cause them pain?

12 Can insects make you ill?

Although millions of people do eat insects, there are many reasons to be careful about insect consumption.

1. Insects, like lots of species, can contain toxins or carry bacteria picked up from when the insects fed on rotting food or dead animals. The toxins might not be harmful to humans in small quantities but in larger quantities, they could make you ill if not removed or treated.

2. If you don't eat insects regularly, then a sudden change to eating them may be a shock to your digestive system. Also, if you are allergic to certain foods (for example, shellfish) then you might be allergic to particular insects (crickets are also **arthropods** like crabs or lobsters).

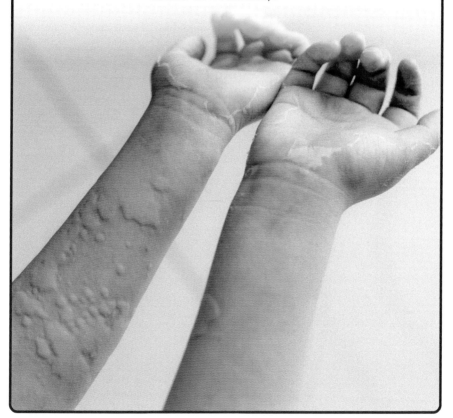

3. The way in which insect food is produced is vital. Like any other food, producers may use harmful chemicals to kill pests (like other insects!) or germs. In time, we may find out which methods are the safest and cleanest.

4. The health benefits of eating insects are still not clear. Yes, many contain vitamins, but food experts don't even agree about whether some of these vitamins really improve health (wherever they come from).

13 Worth the price?

You can now find insect dishes at some of the world's top restaurants.

Noma is a Danish restaurant which was voted the second-best restaurant in the world in 2019. In 2012, its owner opened a "pop-up" restaurant in London. A similar one followed in Japan in 2015.

One of the memorable dishes on the menu was ants served on live prawns!

Because of the formic acid inside them, the ants gave a sharp, sour "kick" to the flavour.

But you would need a lot of money to eat a meal like this. The ant dish was part of a menu that cost £225 per person!

14 Turning the tables

Some insects find humans really tasty.

Have you ever woken up to find an itchy red spot on your skin? If so, then you may have been bitten by a mosquito.

Female mosquitoes suck small amounts of blood from people because they need the protein in blood to help develop the eggs they carry.

Researchers have also discovered that mosquitoes drink blood when they are thirsty.

Of course, mosquitoes can cause much more than a nasty itch. In many countries, they pass on a deadly disease called malaria which they have picked up from other human beings.

Other insects which feed off humans include fleas, mites and **midges**.

How can you protect yourself against these bloodsuckers?

You can buy special sprays that the insects don't like. However, these sprays often contain chemicals which are harmful to the environment, so it may be better to avoid them altogether. For example, insects are commonly found where there is standing water, such as a puddle or pond.

In some parts of the world, people have to sleep with special nets around their beds to keep mosquitoes out.

Cleaning up food waste and other rubbish also helps keep them away.

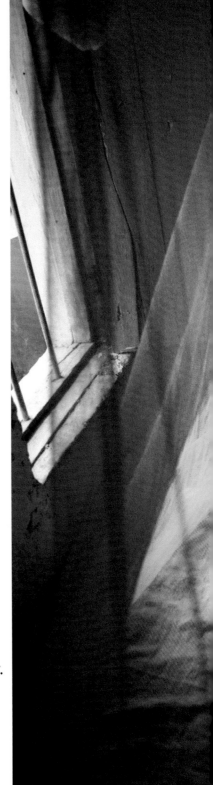

15 What do you think?

In many stories, insects are presented as horrible creepy-crawlies. However, this book has shown that there are lots of people who enjoy eating insects. Perhaps you are one of them. Many people also believe insects are nutritious and farming them could be good for the environment.

What do you think? Will eating insects one day be as common as eating rice or bread?

Whatever *you* believe, don't go out and start digging up the garden looking for your next meal. Knowing which insects are safe to eat is for the experts.

Glossary

arthropods animals with jointed limbs and a body made up of segments

calories measure of energy

carbohydrate source of food and energy for animals

devour eat enthusiastically

larvae newly hatched form of many insects

maggots legless larvae of a fly or other insect

midges tiny biting flies; unlike mosquitoes, they don't carry disease

nutrients substances that help living things grow

protein food that a body's cells need for growth and repair

scrub land which is a mix of open fields, plants and trees

supplements extra food or nutrients

sustainable keeping an ecological balance

toxins poisons

Index

Eating insects

Benefits
1. Tasty – lots of flavours and textures, from spicy to sweet
2. Nutritious – lots of vitamins
3. Readily available
4. Could reduce need for intensive farming
5. Lots of people eat them all around the world as an alternative to beef and chicken, for example

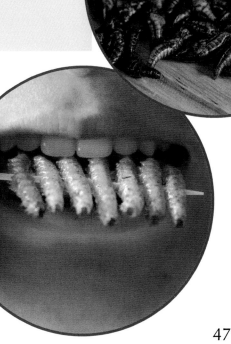

Challenges

1. Not everyone likes the flavours or feel of them

2. Some contain toxins and bacteria

3. Lots needed to mass-produce food

4. Still need to be farmed so use a lot of energy

5. Insects are animals so vegetarians can't eat them

❖ Ideas for reading ❖

Written by Gill Matthews
Primary Literacy Consultant

Reading objectives:
- check that the text makes sense to them, discuss their understanding and explain the meaning of words in context
- ask questions to improve their understanding of a text
- identify main ideas drawn from more than one paragraph and summarise these
- retrieve and record information from non-fiction

Spoken language objectives:
- ask relevant questions to extend their understanding and knowledge
- use relevant strategies to build their vocabulary
- articulate and justify answers, arguments and opinions

Curriculum links: Science – Living things and their habitats

Interest words: protect, harmful, commonly

Resources: IT

Build a context for reading
- Ask children to look at the front cover and to read the title. Ask what it means to them.
- Read the back-cover blurb. Explore how the children feel about eating insects. How do they think eating insects could solve the world's problems? Encourage children to support their responses with reasons.
- Point out that this is an information book. Explore children's knowledge of the features of non-fiction books, e.g. contents, glossary, index. Give them time to skim the book to find these features. Discuss their purpose and organisation.

Understand and apply reading strategies
- Ask children to use the contents page to find the chapter called *Insects on the menu*. Read pp2–5 aloud. Discuss the questions at the beginning and end of the chapter.
- Read pp6–9. Demonstrate how to identify the main ideas in each paragraph to summarise the information given in the chapter.